THExPERT LEADER

USING THE HUMAN EXPERIENCE TO LEAD AT THE NEXT LEVEL

MICHAEL E. PERRY, Ph.D.

Copyright © 2018 by Michael E. Perry, Ph.D.

All rights reserved. No part of this book may be used or reproduced or transmitted in any form or in any manner whatsoever, electronic or mechanical, including photocopying, recording, or by any information storage and retrieval system, without written permission except in the case of brief quotations embodied in critical articles or reviews.

Book and Cover design by C.E.A.D.

For information contact :
Catalyst Executive Advising and Development, LLC Evans, GA
www.connectmovegrow.com

CHAPTER ONE

The Catalyst Human Experience Concept (HEx)

FOR TOO LONG, the practice and art of working effectively with people has often been discounted as "soft" or "fluffy" and relegated to realm of optional skills...after all the "important" leader skills have been mastered. In an effort to discover new ways of understanding and motivating people, leaders have searched for what they consider "hard" scientific explanations, often in the form of the latest empirically based research literature. It's a great place to start, but it's only the beginning. Some leaders seek "scientific" explanations and approaches in search of straightforward tools that provide an escape from the complex and nuanced factors associated with frequent person-to-person interaction. Let's face it...people are complicated. Here's the catch. Dismissing effective engagement with people (the ability to effectively motivate, connect, and communicate) as "soft skills" and thereby unimportant, is to ignore over a century of established scientific work that continues to build our understanding of human thinking, behavior, and social interaction. In fact, we have long known that our day-to-day experience is a complex interaction of our biology, psychology, social interactions, and environment.

By the way, if you've ever wondered about the where the term "soft skills" originated, you will find it in a 1972 report prepared by the United States Army. Surprised? The topic? Establishing effective methods for determining "soft skill" job requirements for leaders—that is, roles that required working with *people*, rather than machines.

That's right. The term actually had nothing to do with scientific rigor. It was a practical way to describe work that was inherently people-related. Even in 1972, Army researchers and leaders knew that the key to enhancing people's work performance was...you guessed it...other people. The *military* knew that in 1972. How are we doing now, in present-day?

For leaders, it is absolutely essential that <u>people</u> are their priority, no matter the organization and the function that organization performs. Leaders have the ability to shape culture and impact people's experiences in quite profound ways. The experience that leaders create can lead to increased job satisfaction, better productivity, and increased profits; or conversely, dissatisfaction, conflict, and employee turnover.

Leaders have the profound ability to influence the world around them. Despite the impact they leverage, leaders are commonly unaware of the depth of individual and collective experiences around them and how they might shape those experiences. There is a constant flurry of activity, response, and adaptation occurring in and around every human being—**the human experience**. Leaders can impact that experience, directly or indirectly. With a very basic understanding of the components of the human experience, a leader can change everything.

The Catalyst Human Experience (HEx) Model accounts for the complex convergence of the **Biological, Social, Environmental, and Cognitive** building blocks of human behavior...the Human Experience (HEx). Leaders who understand the human experience can shape, motivate, and respond to their people in ways that transform teams and promote performance that is beyond expectations.

Human beings are extraordinarily complex creatures, and there is much that science has yet to discover. Given that reality, it is obviously not the intent of this publication to prepare you for medical or psychological practice! What this publication will do, however, is provide leaders with a fresh perspective and a starting point on the seemingly countless ways they can begin to understand, influence, and leverage the full range of the human experience—Biological, Cognitive, Social, and Environmental.

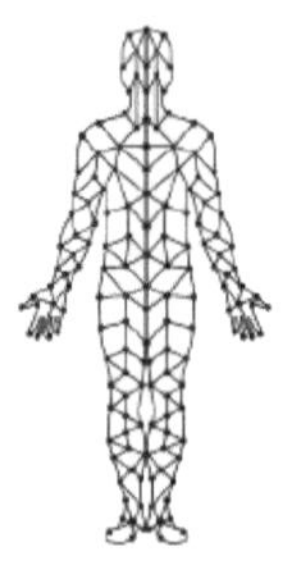

CHAPTER TWO

BIOLOGICAL

ALTHOUGH IT IS NOT IMMEDIATELY APPARENT, leadership affects biology. Surprised? It is unlikely that most leaders consider that their words, actions, and decisions might alter the biology of other human beings, but that is exactly the case. Read on...

Biology includes some fixed factors, such as sex, age, and genetic makeup. Biological factors also include things like physical health, nutrition, and physical needs. We'll focus most our brief journey on the biology of the brain. For now, we will focus most of our brief journey on the bilogy of our body's central control center-the brain.

Leaders can impact the function and structure of people's brains. You read that right. There are several ways that leaders can actually influence the way the brain works and develops, ultimately influencing emotions and behavior.

Among the most compelling biological components of the human experience are neurotransmitters, also known as hormones. Hormones are stimulated based on real or perceived triggers in the environment, stimulating responses such as excitement, fear, satisfaction, happiness, connection and many others.

Hormones are <u>real,</u> and their job is to transmit messages and drive behavior. Hormones are the biological building blocks of human behavior. The following illustration lists several well-known neurotransmitters and their role in shaping human behavior.

NEUROTRANSMITTERS	
ADRENALINE **fight or flight** Produced in stressful situations. Increases heart rate and blood flow. Leads to physical boost and heightened awareness	**CORTISOL** **stress** Mediates stress response. Regulates blood pressure. Increases blood sugar (glucose). Controls sleep/wake cycle. Boosts energy to handle stress and restore balance.
OXYTOXIN **connection** Shown to increase trust, altruism, and bonding. Can promote a strong sense of contentment.	**SEROTONIN** **mood** Contributes to well-being and happiness. Helps sleep cycle and digestive system regulation. Affected by exercise and light exposure.
DOPAMINE **reward/pleasure** Feelings of pleasure, also addiction, movement and motivation. People repeat behaviors that lead to dopamine release.	**ENDORPHINS** **euphoria** Released during exercise and excitement, producing well-being and euphoria. Reduces pain.

How do leadership decisions and behavior influence hormones? (An important note: The body's production and distribution of neurotransmitters is a profoundly complex and intricate process. None of the body's systems function in isolation. The descriptions provided here are designed provide a straight forward way of describing the role of neurotransmitters in human behavior; however, readers should understand that multiple factors (often unknown) can contribute to mood and behavior. It is important to avoid over-simplification of neurochemical processes when attempting to practically apply this information.)

Adrenaline—The primary catalyst of the "fight or flight" response. Adrenaline increases heart rate and blood flow to boost physical capability and heighten awareness. It is triggered in times of excitement and fear. Adrenaline can be stimulated by great news or threats to life or livelihood. *A shot of adrenaline can get the heart pounding almost immediately as the body prepares to react to something...NOW! Even simple word choices can trigger very strong physiological reactions—positive or negative.*

Dopamine—Associated with feelings of pleasure and stimulates motivation and movement. Dopamine is all about reward. People repeat behaviors that lead to the release of dopamine. Dopamine release can be stimulated by food, drink, drugs, visually appealing items, and even recognition and acknowledgement!

Leaders who know what motivates their people can be master influencers. When reward comes in the form that the recipient finds valuable and appealing, repeat behavior is much more likely to follow.

Serotonin—Related to feelings of well-being and good mood. Release of serotonin can be triggered by feeling wanted, important, proud, and other positive mindsets. Serotonin is more of a slow acting neurotransmitter, meaning that any change in levels is more a result of cumulative experiences versus singular events. A culture of appreciation and inclusion might increase serotonin levels among a group of people over time, resulting in a generally more positive environment. People who feel unappreciated or worthless may have lower levels of serotonin and, as a result, lower mood states.

Oxytocin—Released in response to warm connection with others and trust. Oxytocin is the hormone behind people's natural tendency to feel close to babies and puppies! Workplaces that foster intimate connection and genuine relationships benefit from the human connection promoted by oxytocin. *Think of that feeling you get when you see a military service member reunite with their family after a year-long deployment! Say thanks to oxytocin. What types of behaviors promote that feeling on a day-to-day basis at the workplace?*

Cortisol—Released in response to stress. Manages the body's release of fuel, regulates blood pressure, controls sleep cycles, and boosts energy. Designed to function over the short term. *If stressors like job security, being singled out, and fear of loss are the order of the day,* *the short-term impact of Cortisol can be any number of reactionary behaviors, including rushing to judgement, lack of creativity, and flawed decision making. Over the long term, the result of a stressful work environment can be adverse physical consequences, like high blood pressure, heart disease, and organ problems.*

Endorphins—Naturally produced stimulants that activate good feelings—even euphoria. Endorphins provide a "second wind" that helps you to push through challenges by reducing pain/discomfort and fatigue. Endorphins can also stimulate a sense of achievement. *In the past, the most commonly recognized source of endorphin release was prolonged strenuous exercise—running, in particular. The "runner's high" is a phenomenon that many of us have heard of, but few have experienced. The good news is that we don't have to run a marathon to experience endorphin release. Believe it or not, laughter among a group of people has been shown to release endorphins in the brain! Think about it. The last time you heard a great joke, saw a great comedy routine, or laughed with friends, what were you focused on? Probably not stress, problems, or pain.*

There is no doubt that hormones are powerful mediators of behavior, but the human body is capable of much more. Until recent decades, scientists thought that our brains were pretty-much fixed and fully developed once we reached adulthood. Ever heard the phrase, "can't teach an old dog new tricks"? As it turns out, advances in science have shown us that our brains constantly adapt throughout our lives.

The most amazing thing about the brain is its ability to continue creating new pathways for learning and development, well into our senior years. Modern developments in neurological research have dispelled previous notions that the brain only grew and changed during childhood. The brain's ability to continue responding and adapting to new challenges is referred to as "neuroplasticity." The STRUCTURE of our brains actually can and does change!

The brain is made up of tens of billions of specialized cell structures called neurons. Electrical impulses carry information through neurons, and neurotransmitters (remember them?) and carry information chemically between neurons. Whenever we think, feel, or do something, information travels along a series of neurons. We call these neuropathways. Neuropathways that are well established are like well-worn trails. They are familiar and often automatic. Think if these as habits. The interesting thing is that neurotransmitters—and therefore habits—can be altered. This is the essence of neuroplasticity. Every time we try a new behavior or a new way of thinking, we create a new neuropathway. The more we practice that new behavior or way of thinking, the stronger the neuropathway becomes and the more automatic the behavior and/or thinking becomes.

*What does all of this have to do with **Leadership**?*

If you are a leader, you have a direct influence on the biological responses of the people you lead. You can influence mood and behavior, and you also can literally change people's brains by changing their experiences or challenging them to learn new things. But get this...every time a leader micromanages, fails to delegate, or withholds vital information, the opportunity for new neuropathways, learning, and behavior is lost.

CHAPTER THREE

COGNITIVE

LEADERS WHO UNDERSTAND THE POWER of cognitive factors appreciate their capacity to shape the world that their teams work in. Cognition involves acquiring knowledge and making sense out of the world. Through a complex and ever evolving integration of thoughts, environment, sensory information, problem solving, calculation, evaluation, decision making, etc., cognitive processes build on our understanding of people and things around us. Cognitive factors are also the catalyst for things like mood, values, beliefs, bias, motivation, perception, etc. Our brain and body are in a constant state of responding to the world around us. Most of us might believe that our responses to life's situations are automatic reactions to our current circumstances. That is only partially true. A common way of thinking is that situations trigger emotions, which then impact the subsequent behavior. The following illustration details the way that most people see this flow of events:

Cognition represents not only the function of our brain, but also the way in which we make meaning of our world and experiences. The problem with the traditional way of thinking about behavior is that we omit several vital components of the cognitive process—past experiences, beliefs, and automatic thoughts. Considering the influence of these three variables on cognition helps us to begin to understand how two people might experience the exact same situation but have very different emotions and responses. The following illustration represents a more complete picture of the flow of events that shape emotion and behavior:

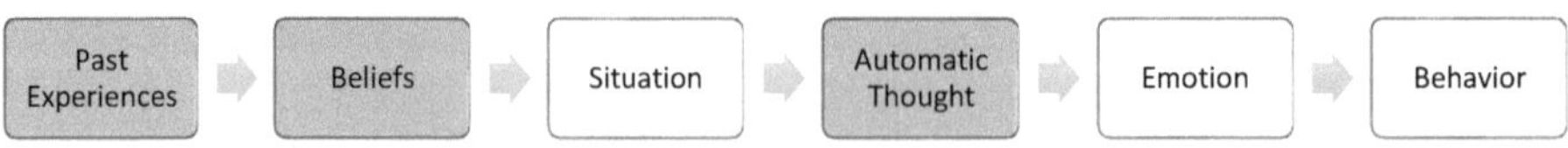

People generally respond to situations from a certain perspective and context. Perspective is shaped, in part, through past experiences. As we accumulate experiences and acquire beliefs, we develop a filter, of sorts, that we run all situations through. What that filter captures is very much influenced by what we have learned over time. Once a situation has been run through our filter, we assess what that situation means...usually automatically. Those are our automatic thoughts—also known as "judgements" or perceptions of situations. Our emotions flow from those judgements and perceptions. If our perceptions and automatic thoughts are positive, then positive emotions and productive behavior tend to follow. On the other hand, if we perceive situations negatively based on negative automatic thoughts, negative emotions and non-productive behavior are often the result.

Leaders are not mind-readers, nor can they change the past. However, it is critically important to understand that there is an underlying cognitive process working in every single person. Two people can experience an identical situation and have completely divergent responses. That divergence is very often based in cognition— the meaning we make of the world, based on past experiences and firmly held beliefs. The good news is that beliefs can shift with new experiences, and automatic thoughts can be challenged and adjusted, based on current reality.

Here is a relevant example (this is based on a true scenario).

A new leader in an academic institution assumed a position previously occupied by someone with an oppressive and micromanaging leadership style. For several years, members of the team were given strict limits on their work roles and criticized harshly for mistakes. There were some who even lost their jobs because they spoke out in opposition to the leadership of that time. The culture was established and the beliefs about leadership were etched in.

The new leader inherited this team...and their baggage. Although the new leader was fair and open to new ideas and even disagreement, many months passed before the team's **new experiences**, shifted their **beliefs** about leadership and changed their automatic thoughts about situations. The shift required months of consistently fair behavior and decision making. As a result, the general emotional tone and behaviors completely shifted, resulting in more involvement, discussion, and creativity over time—in this case, more than a year.

*What does all of this have to do with **Leadership**?*

Understand that people's emotions, decisions, and behavior are shaped by a complex convergence of experiences. What you do and say in leadership adds to those experiences and shapes how your team thinks about you, each other, and the roles they perform. There are times when leaders must fix things they did not break. People are wired to protect themselves and survive. When leaders are interacting with team members who have beliefs and responses based on negative past situations, it might take time and consistency to reshape the culture and overall mindset. New experiences create new neuropathways of thought, emotion and behavior. With consistency and repetition, new habits follow and become automatic, establishing a culture that, at its best, yields higher job satisfaction and increased productivity, which have a direct, positive impact on profitability. Taking care of your front line takescare of the bottom line.

CHAPTER FOUR

SOCIAL

LEADERS CAN DIRECTLY IMPACT the nature of social interaction in the organization, and as such, they possess a remarkable capacity to shape the experience of their entire organization through the relationships they facilitate and cultivate. Social factors involve the relationship between each individual and the people around them. Human interaction, relationship formation, group dynamics, influence, discipline, and other factors are all examples of social influences that shape our daily experience.

Humans are inherently relational beings. Our thoughts, feelings, and behaviors are influenced by the actual or perceived presence of others. Although we each carry unique preferences and traits, most people function more effectively when they can interact with others in some way. Human interaction makes possible a broad range of possibilities, including vicarious learning (by watching), collective intelligence, and modeling of behavior. Leaders have a powerful opportunity to set the stage for human interaction in their organizations. As organizational norms are established and reinforced, seasoned veterans and newcomers alike more easily discover and embrace "who *we* are and what *we* do" in the places they work.

One great way to build relationships and mutually beneficial social interactions is to establish a values-based approach to leadership. From an organizational perspective, values define the beliefs, standards, and behavior that drive business practices, relationships, and decisions. Leading with values gives current and prospective team members a clear picture of what the organization believes and stands for. Most individuals have a personal set of values that shape how they see and interact with the world. To the extent that there is a commonality, overlap, and understanding of the organization's values and the values of the individuals it employs, there is a greater opportunity to create a more unified, effective, and loyal team. The idea is not to create "clones," but rather to be clear about what is most important to the organization and the team. This approach reduces some effort by allowing prospective team members to determine if they might be a good fit for a particular employer before they even say "yes" to that new position. The key idea is to bring together a team of unique people and fresh ideas to accomplish more collectively than can be accomplish individually.

What does all of this have to do with **Leadership**?

Effective leaders recognize that their own fate and the destiny of their organization are dependent on a group of people who must work together effectively. The values driving the organization combined with the values that the team brings to the table will go a long way toward creating the ideal social environment. The expectations and norms the leader puts into place are also vitally important.

Does your organization value collaboration between people or promote competition?

Does your culture encourage connection or reinforce separation?

Is conflict between people managed promptly and effectively, or has controversy and tension become commonplace?

No matter what your organization does, people are your first mission. Discover ways to leverage their common values, unique perspectives and collective wisdom, and you will experience the true power of teamwork. That's what social interaction is all about.

CHAPTER FIVE

ENVIRONMENTAL

ENVIRONMENT IS ONE FACTOR that leaders can have almost direct impact on shaping. Environmental considerations include tangible, physical things like furnishings, work area design, and amenities. Environment also includes geographical location, climate, and community. Culture—that is, organizational culture—can also shape the environment that people experience when at their place of work. Leaders can certainly dictate the culture within an organization as they dictate their team's experience within the culture. Organizational culture is arguably the most important environmental variable. Culture represents the attitudes and behavioral characteristics commonly demonstrated in the workplace. Leaders have profound influence on the organizational culture that impacts the experience of those working in their organizations. Fortunately, culture is a variable that leaders can shape from day one.

Unlike furniture, amenities, and even human-centered design elements, culture cannot be purchased, nor can it be manufactured. Culture influences the environment in a way that is often invisible to the eye, but quite tangible in terms of how people feel in a certain place. Have a culture that encourages communication and trust? Creativity is likely to follow. Have zero-defects expectations in a setting where mistakes are inevitable? Expect high stress and unmet potential. Have a culture that pits peers against each other to determine "winners" and "losers"? Expect poor teamwork, low collaboration, and stagnant organizational growth. The tone and feel of culture either provide a boost or serve as detriment to other elements of an organization's environment.

Culture's importance is undeniable, but the remaining elements of the environment cannot be ignored. For example, people are more productive in spaces they consider comfortable. Consideration of chairs, desks, lighting, and all things physical are quite important. Believe it or not, proper lighting can improve energy, mood, and performance. Careful planning of work areas and furniture can have a direct impact on the morale and health of your team. Standing desks have grown in popularity, because there can be long term negative health consequences when most of the work day is spent in a seating position. (Note: The health benefits of standing desks are a point of some debate, with some studies revealing negative health consequences of standing for long periods. It seems that whether you stand or sit, movement is the key to improving your health. That is for another publication. Increased rates of obesity, higher blood pressure, abnormal cholesterol levels, and overall increased risk of death from cardiovascular disease and cancer are among those consequences. Fortunately, increasing numbers of employers are considering the long-term health impact of the environments they establish, and they are working to make a difference.

Companies like Facebook, Samsung, LinkedIn, and other tech giants have placed environmental features at the top of their priority list in recent years. Innovative features include vast continuous office floors, biospheres, glass walls with mountain views, copious sunlight, putting greens, lush outdoor terraces, indoor tents, rooftop parks, team pods with snacks and drinks, and countless other features and aminities. These are only a few of the environmental touches incorporated in many of these west-coast based technology companies that make possible so many of our communication and information platforms. Given the stiff competition for talent in the tech sector, these companies are fighting to remain on the leading edge of creating spaces that incorporate elements employees desire, making it easier, and even more enjoyable for them to do their best work.

It might be difficult, impractical, or impossible for you to get that rooftop park into the budget this year...or ever. That's okay. The important thing to consider here is that environment matters. Whether you are creating spaces for more seamless interaction, or providing places where people can think, eat, or rest, the environment can make the difference in morale, productivity, engagement, and satisfaction.

What does all of this have to do with **Leadership**?

Leaders establish the cultural tone of the environment through their words, attitude, and actions. Similarly, leaders form the physical appearance and function of the environment through their understanding of human psychology, optimal work conditions, and health needs. The reality is that tech companies are not alone. Most employers are having to consider new ways to appeal to an emerging workforce populated by people who have numerous attractive options. The cost of creating optimal work environments is, no doubt, a deterrent to many organizations. But the question they must ask is, "Can we afford NOT to invest in people in this way?" Overlooking the environment will reap a benefit or exact a cost, typically in the form of attracting top talent or losing invaluable institutional expertise.

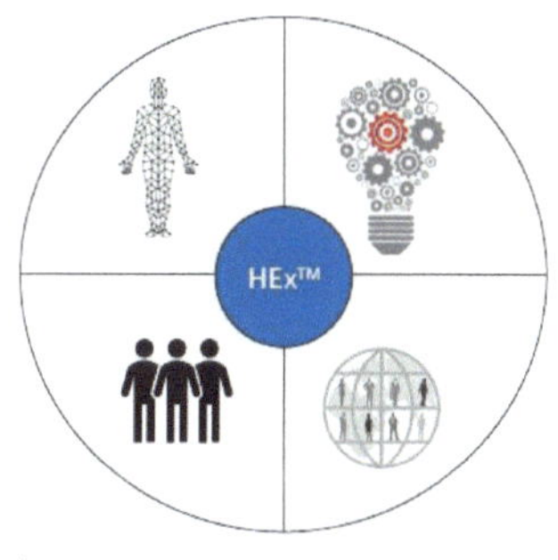

C H A P T E R   S I X

THE MODEL

THESE FOUR COMPONENTS OF HUMAN EXPERIENCE provide points of understanding and intervention for leaders seeking to more effectively shape the experience of their teams. The components tie together thoughts, relationships, biological functions, and environmental factors in a complex but modifiable series of interactions. For leaders who recognize the impact of their behavior and the opportunity to impact the behavior of others, there is boundless opportunity to unleash unlimited potential.

The Catalyst Human Experience (HEx) Model™

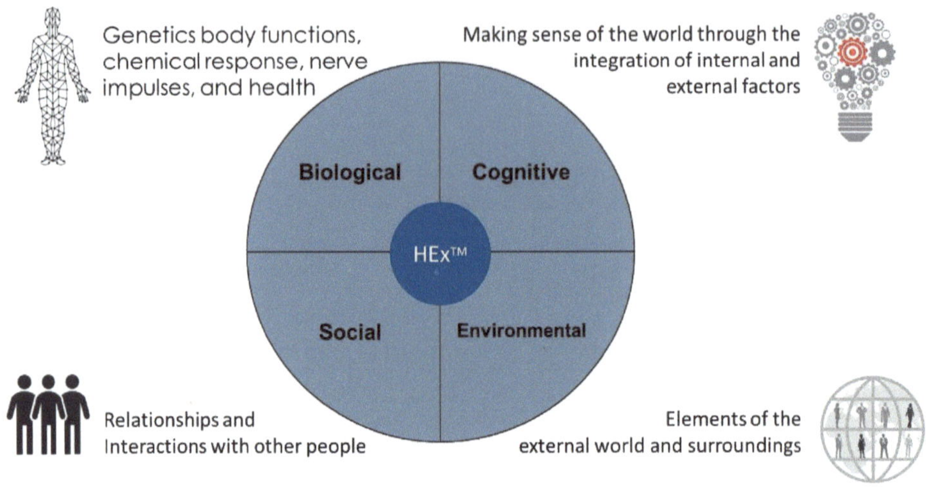

Every human being experiences the world in a unique way. Every. Single. One. Leaders who understand the full range of the human experience are better equipped to respond in ways that matter for themselves and others. This level of understanding creates a distinct leadership advantage. The Catalyst Human Experience (HEx) Model™ is the foundation of how we understand people and help leaders to not only understand, but to inspire, motivate, and get the results that make the difference.

PUTTING IT INTO ACTION

HEx QUESTIONS for Leaders to Consider

1. Biological

    a. What neurotransmitters might be most often triggered in our organization? Do we need change?

    b. How might my behaviors promote or inhibit the creation of new neuropathways for each member of the team?

2. Cognitive

    a. What do I want my team's perception and judgment to be regarding their current leadership? What automatic thoughts do I want to encourage? What emotions and behaviors will follow?

    b. Are there "broken" things our team has been affected by that I need to help repair, although I did not break them?

3. Social

    a. What are the top three commonly held values of my team?

    b. If I had to evaluate our team cohesion on 10-point scale (1-worst, 10-best), we would receive a _____.
    Our score for effectively managing conflict is _____.
    Do we need change?

4. Environmental

    a. I would use the following words to describe our culture:
    ____

    b. What investments do I need to make to enhance our environment and improve the work environment?

About the Author

Mike Perry is a Clinical Psychologist, Leadership Consultant, Leadership Coach, Trainer, and retired Army Officer. During his military service of over 21 years, Mike held various leadership positions in the US and abroad. His extensive experience in leadership and human performance is coupled with a passion for helping leaders to drive meaningful change and create unified culture. Mike is a graduate of Norfolk State University, Norfolk, VA. He holds a Ph.D. degree in Clinical Psychology and a Master of Science Degree in Medical Psychology from the Uniformed Services University of the Health Sciences in Bethesda, Maryland. He is also a graduate of Georgetown University's Leadership Coaching Certification Program.

If you have found the information in this book helpful please leave a book review. Be sure to follow us on **Facebook** and **Instagram @catalyst706**.

www.CONNECTMOVEGROW.com

Who We Are and What We Believe

Catalyst Executive Advising & Development (CEAD)* specializes in developing leaders and shaping organizational culture. We are a seasoned team of professionals with expertise in Leadership Development, Executive Coaching, Healthcare Administration, and Military to Civilian transition /integration, prepared to help transform your organization and maximize your individual and collective effectiveness.

Catalyst is a business founded with a passion for service to others. We believe that genuine relationships are the cornerstone of our existence and success. Placing people first sets the stage for unimaginable accomplishments. We also believe that trust is the bonding agent for any successful team. Trust is established with integrity, commitment, and consistency. We strive daily to demonstrate these qualities within our company and in every interaction with our clients.

*CEAD is also the parent company of Catalyst Human Performance Experts—providing performance enhancement and psychological services for individuals and groups.

www.CONNECTMOVEGROW.com

One last thing to know, before you go...

At Catalyst Executive Advising & Development, we want to help you to become a better leader...a more effective leader. We believe that our genuine care for people, second-to-none training and expertise, and decades of proven leadership experience have been the difference-makers for us that have equipped us to help make a difference for you. If you would like to know more about how our coaching and leader development services can help remove long-standing obstacles and take your organization to the next level, you can take one of these steps today:

-Schedule a free 30-minute consultation with us by visiting our website at www.connectmovegrow.com.

-Obtain more information about our full line of services on our website at www.connectmovegrow.com.

-Have a question that won't wait? Give us a call at 706-862-1208.

We look forward to hearing from you.

...It starts here!

The Catalyst Team

www.ingramcontent.com/pod-product-compliance
Lightning Source LLC
Chambersburg PA
CBHW040319240726
48664CB00006B/1552